Ice Box: Rebound & Recover

By: Ra'Mone Marquis

Ice Box: Rebound & Recover

A Novel Written by:
Ra'Mone Marquis

Copyright © 2021 by Ra'Mone Marquis
Published by: Tru Phoenix, LLC.

Cover Design: Derrick Vaughan/Sphinx Imaging, LLC.
Editor: Tru Phoenix, LLC.

Table of Contents

Book Dedication

I could tell you everything. I may get a lecture, but I got love and not judgement. You gave me a safe place to always be able to come to. You consistently built me up and had my back. There was no gossiping about me from you. You kept my secrets and shadowed me with unconditional love. Beyond the materialistic things and unending support, what significantly made our bond so deep, was your constant desire to protect my heart. You rescued me as a young child and loved me through traumas. I have been successful in a variety of ways , because you instilled in me every single thing I needed to make it in life…..except for how to live life without you. You forever are my heart and my everything!

R.I.H.

Amanda Burnette Fluellen

"Granny"

11-36-39/6-5-2019

Broken Architect #1

They've said your grace is sufficient

My pain seems to be highly sustainable

I am crippled by it

I am awakened by it

Manifesting physically

Often unable to move

All parts of me broken down

You knew I was at the edge dangling over

Barely holding on

You scattered the already scattered

You broke the already broken

You're sprinkling droplets reminding me

Of your capabilities..desires

You sporadically appeared at the tunnel's end

Feeling abandoned, forgotten, dumb

You walked beside me and comforted me

You kept me

You elevated me

Or did you?

Was I wrong?

Bamboozled

Lost

Confused

Numb and depleted

I slowly felt myself molding

Consumed with fear, anger, embarrassment

I wasn't defeated or broken anymore...

...so I thought

Clearly I lied to myself

I was told that you don't neglect your faithful

Abiding under your shadow

Risks battled with confidence

Led to better days

Like a thief in the night

As swift as I can blink my eyes

You took your hand off me

Buried my partial heart and destroyed my soul.

Exhale: Where Are You?

You know what I remember when I learned how to exhale

I could exhale and all my problems evaporated

There's a peace that would come over me

It would soothe me

Over powering strength would guide me

When I learned how to exhale

My face didn't just smile - my heart did

Foreign territory…I embraced it

A door wasn't opened to self-love

The need for folks' validation was vacated

Evolution occurred

Growth broadened

Consistency with my joys and passions

Healing and brokenness was strong

Damn near choked me a few times

Healing intersected that alleviation widespread

Infectious livelihood

Exuded a transformation

Modified journey ensured

I remembered how to exhale

Past tense

Unable to breathe

There's no in and out

Breath snatched out of my body

Soul snatched..disappeared from me

Like smoke from a blunt

I'm left crippled

Unrecognizable in the mirror

Lifeless and lost in the middle of an intersection

Alone and unguided…

…if only I could exhale.

Attention Pain

I just want the pain to stop

That's something I've told myself quite often

A seed that grew

Watered by fear and anger

Mistakes and depression

Loneliness and disappointment

Pain

Pain with no gain has seemed to be the objective

Stunted healing

The heart is numb

I've had moments where joy and progression seemed to visit me

Why was it hindered?

Trusted the wrong people – sure

Kept the wrong company – I'll take that

Alcohol – hard pill to swallow but I had no choice

When hard work is the focus

Self-control is in the driver's seat

People cleanse refreshes me

Dedication to service heals me partially

It wasn't enough

Afraid to call on him

Embarrassed

Praying yearned for

No right words found – empty

No more in sync

My heart yearns for something my brain finds taboo

I just want the pain to stop

My family doesn't give a damn

Trusted friends scarce and not local

Unappreciated

Overused

Misunderstood

Ignored

I just want it fixed

How much broken can a broken heart be

No boomerang has brought good fortune my way

Cupid skips over me

Jolly old St. Nick I could care less about

Release me…rebuild me

Cover me…fill me

I no longer know if my cup is half empty

I no longer know if my cup runneth over

The cup no longer exists…period

I have to move on

I'm expected to replenish strength

Sustained at empty

I've rectified, modified, and simplified

The brokenness, bruising, loneliness, inadequate guilt

Makes me disintegrated and paralyzed

The pain is sustainable

Emotionally and mentally paraplegic

Spiritually disabled

It all just hurts…daily

Consistently feeling as if I'm fighting a losing battle

I hope for more

Wishing I had something…I need something to live for

My biggest source of power and love

Has become the centerpiece of my pain and guilt

Sorrow and fears

Demotivation and devastation

She taught me well…taught me everything

The faith instilled is very strong

The pain allowed is winning

I'm tired, done, exhausted

Salute to pain

I see now…it's time to throw in the towel.

Amanda

There's a wind that blows when I think of you

Overcome with loneliness and comfort

My spirit is bruised

My heart is broken

You were always the wind beneath my wings

Your prayers saved me from a far

Your words made my heart sing and dance

Your love and teachings made my possibilities limitless

You were always my everything

You were always my heart

Lost and damaged

I'm in the middle of an intersection

I don't know which road to go down

Parent unit abandoned and neglected me

You stepped in and saved me

You did what was best

For that I'm blessed

Success of failure

You didn't do anything that

Didn't have my best interest at heart

Broadened horizons

Name brand labels

Nurtured talents

You upheld me when everything around me failed

When in the late night hour

Trouble vexed me

You answered…words soothed the hurricane inside

Tornado of emotions

By conversation's end

It was as if God himself spoke through you

And said peace be still

You were my guardian angel

You loved me

Soothed me

Bonded with me

A magnet couldn't make us any tighter

My bridge over troubled water

My bridge over the stormy seas of misfortune

You wiped my tears away

Chased my doubts away

You introduced me to HIM

When my foundation was unstable

I had faith 'cause you believed

Aware of how HE kept you

Your faith in HIM

My faith in you

Me? A version of a prodigal son

I never strayed too far from his still small voice

There isn't one thing I wouldn't be willing

To give up to have you back

If God was willing to swap

Multiple candidates I could give instead of you

You celebrated my accomplishments

You fed me and my heart's desire

My character and integrity

You molded and nurtured

Many times this body of mine let me down

You held my hand

No matter how far

You remained by my side

Whenever I reached out to you

You were never not there

Past surgery

You were broken 'cause you couldn't take the pain away

You helped carry my burdens

You helped carry my pain

Far from suicidal

I just don't want to continue with life

You died

A large chunk of me died too

The hole left still remains

I miss your smile

I miss our gossip

I miss the magic in your hugs

I miss the confidence your prayers gave me

I'm not doing well granny

Life is so hard without you

I still need you

I wish I could've gone with you

Nothing left in me to give

No longer happy or visited by joy

In the dead of the night

I want to run away

Searching and desperate for peace and healing

Looking in the mirror unaware of who I see

At night when the wind blows

I hear you call my name

I open myself

I prepare myself

Longing for the moment you'll visit me

Yet you haven't came

Having taught me well

Having planted many seeds

I know at some point I'll flourish again

With half of your faith and strength

I know the sun will shine again

Seeing the best in me

Touched my hand

Made me untouchable

Made me see a lot of truths

Helped my dreams come true

While overflowing my life with joy

I am who I am because you loved me

You never falted…open-minded and strong

Wise and graceful

A source of all things good

You were one of the few positive beings

In a hugely negative world

Rest on my queen

You struggled…you overcame

You prayed…you fasted

You loved me unconditionally

You endured turmoil and strife

Patience was bar one

It's the twinkle in your eyes for me

Both reassurance and a sign

There was a plan and anointing you possessed

Purpose fulfilled it was your time

For you to go

Damaged yet optimistic

Hurting but not giving up

Guilty but his grace sufficient

When in those dark moments

Something comes over me

Assuring me that you still got me

Many things I know…many things I do not

One thing I know for sure

I was blessed and highly favored

I was yours and you were mine

I remember heaven's wonder on your face

The love of God in your eyes

79 years visiting this lowly place

Then you returned to your home way above the skies.

Rebound and Recover

Can life be better than before

Will I realize my goals and increase the score

Will folk remember my name

Will they forget due to shame

Rebounding may not be the same

Rules may have changed in this same 'ole game

I can collect the pieces and welcome a new start

Courage and faith keeping me from falling apart

Society is different and changed

What I knew is out of range

I can conquer life and fulfill

I had dreams lost when I got ill

The ride of being well is so long

If I can make it through this

I'll be significantly strong

Depression tried to kill…I survived

An attempt to recover

So far has kept me alive

When I rebound what will I do

Suffered, betrayed, conquered

I saw through

I've taken trips to and from a dark despair

About self…it's past time to care

It's crazy the things I remember

The things I forget

A collage of sorts of happiness and regret

I recall when I messed up

Days consumed with sadness and tears

I forgot a lot of the good small moments

Unknowingly laughter brought along tears

I'd kill to be happy long term

Fighting to move forward and escape the past

My heart could be soothed with elation

Sadness and pain

Ghosts of the past.

A Fall From Grace

Education wasn't an issue

I was brought into the world smart

Whatever special affect I had is gone

I could lay down my life

I'll still not catch a break

When intelligence got me in the door

Personality allowed me to run the room

The man above put it on repeat

I was the good one

I was the fixer

I was the talented one

I was the leader

Sought after and loved

Pre-teens, teens, 20s, half of my 30s

I was the go to

I was an essential package

Fought through abandonment and betrayal

Hospitalizations and suicide attempts

Published a word…winning

Used blessings to benefit others

But the blessed became the broken

Pride and independence betrayed me

Desperation tainted my judgement

Lack of faith threw me into darkness

Mixed with other's perceptions

No longer floating…I was running

Heart of joy became a collection of burnt coal

Rewarding to humiliated

Weakened armor

Unlimited shots

Like a cancer – fear, anger, secrets

Pain breaks down every inch of my body

All functioning is cut off

Shepherd without a flock

Fisherman without a hook

Marriage without love

Boat without a sail

I'm a boy without a home

A man without a soul

I betrayed me

I neglected me

Not a victim

Not 100% to blame

To whom much is given much is required

When I neglected and abandoned self

I ignored and took advantage of HIM

Grace was rewarded

Mercy was an unabolished entity

Essential and yearned for

My crown isn't gone it's suspended

The clock is ticking

Grace visits me sporadically with staccato visits

It never stays

I haven't pushed longer enough

I have fought hard enough

I haven't necessarily given up

The finish line is far but in a bird's eye view

The good 'ole white flag is within arm's reach

Which route will my presence see

Numb, conflicted, with a big void

I can't guarantee that I want to press on…

Lost Hope

A lot of times I had to enjoy life from the sidelines

Watching it leave me behind

Many past times too afraid to let go…to just live

Recently finding myself too demotivated to try

Found myself trying to hide

Not facing things head on

Searching for ways to escape

For most of my life I truly felt

I was here to benefit others

Was years of that

Just a way to run from living for the man in the mirror

I'm saddened and broken at the pains I've had to endure

Lost and too broken to move on

I don't want my life's scars to consume me

Anything to live for is gone

Relationships and folks will be

Disappointing…I can blink my eye and they're gone

Switched up..script switched…promises broken

Bonds renegotiated

There's something I've learned about my journey

My despairs…my pain

I just want to feel loved

I just want to survive

I know I need to conquer my fears…heal…be molded

Forced to face another day

Hurts, pains, mistakes

Washed away with my tears

Hopefully before it's too late and I slip away.

My New Normal

I'm learning what my new normal is

I'm learning how to live

In a new way

Since that day you were taken away

With the things left unsaid

Knowing I got to say them with every tear I shed

By embracing the pain

Knowing that you live on through the memories that remain

Knowing I will never again see your face…on earth

I have peace at times knowing you're in a better place

Knowing you're in God's care

It gives me the strength to move on

Making the pain much easier to bear

I'm learning what my new normal is

I'm learning how to live

Those prayers that got me through a million days

Saying I love you too Ray that turned rain into sunshine

Smile to a frown

Screams into laughter

Magic had to be present in your hugs

A direct touch from heaven

You hugged me and I felt flushed with peace and strength

Your guidance helped me see what's right in a wrong world

Your lectures mold me and provided much needed maintenance

I'm lonely

I'm lost

I feel unloved

I'm learning what my new normal is

I'm learning how to live

I know I won't find anyone to

Love, support, believe in me like you did

But is there any love left down here for me

I learned it may not share bloodline

There's some family bonds that are deep

Ya know there's a few relatives

Who would diminish our bond and connection to being
materialistic

Alleging that you did this for me..you did that for me

You spoiled me

Our bond and connection was so much deeper

What some don't know is

When I was abandoned and neglected

You cleaned me up, loved on me, helped me heal

Every tear you wiped away

Every pain you prayed away

Every doubt you turned into assurance

You broke through all my walls

You nurtured my strength

Rather Africa, Cali, Miami, Puerto Rico

Rather hell, valley, mountain top

My mustard seed never strayed too far

I knew you was somewhere praying for me

Didn't want to live – you helped me give me renewed life

Lost

You helped me find the light

Even if you had to beat me to find it

Literally and figuratively

Our conversations kept a smile on my heart

Pushing through days are a blur

I'm numb

Vision isn't clear

Directions aren't found

Feeling weaponless – there's daily fights to survive

Like the prodigal son…I want to go back home

I want to go back to basics

What waits for me there?

I see a bookshelf full of books

Each book a memory

Each book a lesson taught

A reminder of what you instilled

A reminder of who I am

Above all a reminder of your strength

A reminder of your faith

Our connection isn't gone…it's still very strong

Body is gone but your spirit hasn't deserted me

I have a foundation to lean back on

I have pieces to put back together

Miserable, stressful, hard

Major goals I got to check off to survive

You and HIM been holding me down consistently since

3:45 in the morning on March 8, 1984

Speed ain't never been my friend

Karma, courage, endurance have been

I'm learning what my new normal is

I'm learning how to live

A new way since that day you left

Brokenhearted and kidnapped soul

I'm learning what my new normal is

I'm learning how to live.

Dark Day #1

I heard when I was younger

That it's dark and hell is hot

Hell? It's life work to stay away from

Darkness like rum during spring break consumes me

It kind of became more consistent than a best friend

There every day

There every night

Damn near like an unwanted shadow

I'm like a DV victim

Constantly choked and battered everyday

I don't fight back

I don't want it to end

I've given up…do I deserve this?

Is this the end?

Is this what my destiny was?

Has it only been a matter of time?

Yep…hell yea to all them damn questions

Pointless

I definitely feel it is over anyway

So why try?

Numb…unhealed

Whatever this was preparing me for…I didn't want it

Talents? Take it

Dreams? Kill 'em

Blessings? Give 'em to someone else

I just don't want to feel like I'm choking everyday

Heart hasn't smiled in over a year

Torn and pierced…stuck with devastation

Finding myself wanting it to flow by faster

Get the daily dose of misery over and done

Jack Daniels and wine are on the menu

Drugs and wine my daily menu choices

Over the counter

I'm going to lose anyway

So let's lessen the pain as much as possible

I see an option

Then it flies away like a blue jay

Many hurdles ahead

Not one ability to clear 'em

Given up without even trying

This time finding myself not caring

Unequipped

Demotivated

Alone

Lost

In a fight with Goliath with no rocks or faith

Racing Bolt with no speed

Battling Luther with no voice

1 on 1 with Kobe but no skills

Destroyed

I'll just continue taking part in my daily menu

Not caring

Just wanting to numb the pain

Not caring to wake up from what I hope was a nightmare

I just want to speed up the time

Rush onward the inevitable.

Who Am I?

In front of the mirror

I see my reflection

Who are you

It's a question I ask my reflection daily

Who am I

A question I ask my soul constantly

Who am I…Who have I become

Not myself…anyone but myself

Living in a fantasy to bury the reality

Making myself the mystery

A strong façade disguising the mystery

Empty…but beyond the point of emptiness

Full to the brim with fake confidence

A guard that will never be broken

Because I broke a long time ago

I'm hurting…don't tell anyone

No one needs to know

Don't show or you've failed

Always okay

Always fine

Always on show

The show must go on

It will never stop

The show must not go on

I know it will

I give up

I give up…giving up

I am lost

I don't need to be saved

I need to be found.

Naked Truth 1: Sadness

They say that happiness will find you

I think sadness finds you too

It sneaks up on you in the darkness

Just when you think you've made it through

It opens holes in what was solid ground

The kind you never know are there

Until you go to take another step

And find you're standing over air

The world around you passes by

In blurs of color and sound

Nothing around you making sense

As you continue your plummet down

You can't remember how it started

And you don't know when it will end

But you know that you'd give anything

To stand up on your feet again

Sadness is that feeling

When the falling doesn't stop

It robs your life of meaning

And all the good things that you've got

So when you finally hit rock bottom

And you look back up at the sky

What you once had seems so far away

The only thing left to do is cry

People all yell out for me to save myself

Calling things about happiness, faith, hope

They're too busy with their lives to realize

It'd be a lot faster if they'd just let down a rope.

Dark Day #2

Over this shit dot com

Surrounded by folks

One neutral one irks me

Some I don't like

A few don't want to know

Unsolicited advice is a daily presence

They're unqualified…highly

Many need to learn when to be seen and not heard

Clearly this was a part of HIS plan

This was the only option on the table

Humbled as hell

I've suffered through worse…that's a lie

Days more miserable

Zero control

No leg to stand on

I ignore

No leg to stand on

I say yes when I want to say hell no

No leg to stand on

I smile and laugh when I want to yell and cuss

Though many blessings can come

Out of unwanted environments

Least expedited interactions

I know where the hell I won't be found

When I move on

Gratitude

Lessons – good, bad, indifferent

Will always reside with them

Me, myself, and I will not be

Nor ever often present

When I find peace

If even for a second

I seclude myself and cherish it

When peace returns more consistently

I won't be letting go

Holding on by any means necessary

I toss and I turn

I found an ally to rescue me through

Most dark days…HIM

I feed the HIM part of me daily

Faith fed instead of depression

Devastation and despair met

An open mind and motivation

Though still in the valley

From looking up at the roots

To eye to eye with the tree tops

Dark days visit me

They still meet me

No longer taking up residence

I'm aggravated with random pop ups

With my bipolar ass.

Naked Truth 2: Peace

At this point I don't care about happiness

I don't even know if peace is that reachable

Is striving for either worth it

Are the results of it realistic…to me

An extended amount of time without it

Makes its existence taboo

It's hard for me to say or think of happiness

Just being content I can do

To see contentment and productivity in life

Does happiness and peace need to exist

If so…for how long

It's a staccato experience in my life

A random leap year of feelings

Every day is a battle

Tired, exhausted, numb

Pause

Yea pause

It's what I need the pain to do

Can I get a week

An emotional runaway

Running to something I can't see

What is my price for peace

He can take it all

Unessential friends? Take 'em

Kill 'em

I can't keep going and going

Disconnected

No place of serenity

No safe place

Abandoned, naked, neglected, bruised

Peace evaporating

While my pieces lay scattered with no glue or home

The end is nigh and I welcome him.

Before I Let Go (Unusual & Uncomfortable)

I want to learn who I really am

Those who experience the unusual

Must be willing to endure the uncomfortable

Unusual the other side of uncomfortable

Uncomfortable the filter weeding out

The strong from the weak

Serious from fake

Determined from impulsive

What is my avenue to what's unusual for me

The unknown

The forgotten

I've let go of what's uncomfortable

Hindered evolution

Tainted joy

Cheapened growth

Warped reality

Disguised motivation…deceitful

Unproductive mantras

Hurt people hurt people

Get 'em before they get me

I've missed out on destiny…the unusual

'Cause of my usual

Was it too far from the cross?

Lost my crown

Visits grave…lost resurrection

Lessons lost because I let go

I needed to persevere

Wrong decisions made

I released things I should've kept

Locked wisdom

I quit and wasn't right

A reason to quit doesn't equate a right to

Can't see it but feel it

Something speaking don't quit

Don't give up

Don't walk away

Is my perseverance that strong?

Being a blessing to others

Where has it gotten me?

Covering others…accomplished what

Kept secrets…smiles on their faces

Walking the straight and narrow…focused

Secluded

Dedicated and consistent

I'm at the edge

Feet dangling over

One incident away

From putting THE END at the end of my story

Long before its destined conclusion

Mind in a blender on low

Heart sautéed by what HE's allowed

Ignored while flagged

Unanswered smoke signals

Or am I at the crossroad between unusual and uncomfortable?

Lacking wisdom to know the difference

I need someone to write the vision

I just need someone to make it clear.

Mirror 2 Mirror: Faith

I salute the intent

I salute the purpose

I salute its power and its very essential presence

I'm talking about faith

People call it a belief

People call it tolerance

Faith justified a person

By faith we are sanctified

Experience joy

By faith we became

Condemnation free

Assurance and fulfillment

Without it my efforts are dead

Live by it

Walk by it

Continue in it

Do everything by it

Grow in it

Good works

Combine it with hope and love

What have I lost?

I wonder and look inward

Only my heart

For it lies with you

Only my soul

Lost

Abandoned by my searching self

Only my voice

The unspoken words

Unfelt plea

A loss to articulate

Broken faith

Lost

Can't even find the words to pray

Thankful

I still have you God

You're still waiting for me…

Naked Truth 3: Accountability

I'm not innocent

I'm not a victim

I don't want to wallow in pain

One thing I am is loyal and consistent

I'm thorough and dedicated as hell

I've hurt

I've hurt and betrayed others

Others have hurt and betrayed me

My life was perfectly formed by HIM

I hurt HIM by neglecting me

I've damaged my external

My internal fell by the side of the road

Led by many sexual sins I cheapened my value

Ignoring standards and teachings

I went from crème de la crème to community

Back against the wall desperate as hell

I've broken the 10 commandments and laws of the land

I've lied

I've deceived

I covered for folk

Nothing I wouldn't do to reach any goal

Determined to break the cycle

Persevered to be better than

Money moved and returned

Creative as hell

I'd been the fixer

For others many times over

Trusted the wrong people

Befriended the wrong bruhs

Held on to folks that HE was trying to get me far from

Without a doubt with better friends

Certain situations would not have occurred

Price…I had to pay for trusting folk

More than I trusted HIM

More than I trusted the discernment and strength inside me

Shackled

Judged

Suffocated

Everything crashed down around me

Feeling as if everything and everyone I loved…I lost

Not as bad as the prodigal son

But I allowed folks and pleasures

To have more of me than HE did

Hoping dedication

Feeding spiritual self-daily

Determined to evolve

Determined to grow

Determined to protect my peace and sanity

Determined to listen to his still small voice more

Determined to set boundaries with no exceptions

Anyone who attracts the old me and not the new and improved

Will cease to exist in life…my life

I'm not innocent

I'm not a victim

I'm perfectly flawed

Fighting tooth and nail

To release myself from secrets, pain, guilt

Fighting tooth and nail

To rise out of a life defying hell

I'd do anything to not have to experience again.

When You Left

My heart broke

Not the cliché kind

A pure manifestation of pain

Ripped my soul out of me

The sparkle in my eye left

The confidence your prayers gave me evaporated

I was lost…I am lost

A collage of people surrounding me

A soup of emotions

Some I forgot

Some I could care less

Most I don't trust

Some raining love on me

Reminding me although you're gone

I'm not quite alone

You took a big part of me when you left

Regrouping

Rebuilding

I've been broken down almost to nothing

Molded to be the better version of myself

The self you prayed over

The self you raised

The self you loved unconditionally

You rescued my soul

You rescued my being

Angry as hell…why couldn't he take other folk

I wasn't perfect but I worshipped him

I prayed and prayed

I had progressed

Many bouts of sickness

Multiple hospitalizations shook my life up

Yet I rather go through all of it a million times over

Than to have lost you

Than to have lost you…my soul…my heart

Still needed you so much

I know you're proud of me

'Cause you said it

I yet still know I have a lot of work to do

One foot in front of the other I'm doing it

You're better off than me…hell

I still take meds you don't

You get to hear Whitney and Michael sing live

I never did

When MLK sent out the boycott letters

One came to your residence

You now can fellowship with him a million times over

I missed your cooking

I missed the magic in your hugs

I missed our gossip sessions

I can still hear you say I love you too Ray

I don't know everything

One of the many I do know

I was blessed because I was loved by you

I got the best parts of you while you were here

Others? You left materialistic stuff

Even in death I'm still getting the best parts of you

Strength, presence, direction, calmness, protection

I'm a new me

I have a new normal

Not quite who or what completely that is

You knew what you were doing

I struggle with guilt

I struggle with wondering what your last thoughts of me were

Wondering if they were positive

Hoping you didn't have any regrets or what ifs

You did damn good by me

Don't doubt it for one second

I hope you didn't feel neglected

I loved you to the moon and back

I do believe you knew I was crazy about you

You knew you was number 1 before everyone

You planted seeds that grew and blossomed

Seeds that I didn't realize you had

Planted are blossoming and taking form now

You 'ole crafty woman

You still feeding your handy work

Making sure I grow

Peace and calmness has elevated my breakthrough and shift

You brought me to Randolph and raised me

You sent me to Pelham and healed me.

Dear God (Part 2)

I went against everything you've wanted for me

If I didn't go against it

I ran

I ignored

Neglected myself

Disobeyed you

Abandoned myself

Ran away from your will

Multiple times placed at risk

Battered and broken many times over

I remember when you allowed me to be sick many times

Many times you healed me

How many times?

You have allowed me to feel as if I am at my lowest

Multiple times

Each time lower than the spot before it

Moment of rescue

Reign of freedom

I've been better and stronger

I have struggled with faith

Instead of leaning on your everlasting arm

Desperate times have caused me to make desperate decisions

Who do I turn to for a fix?

I have never strayed too far from your still small voice

I have been afraid of you

I have felt unworthy of your grace

Embarrassed

Guilty

My journey with you has been a seesaw

Many times just you and I

Many times in the dark I've called your name

I've cried

Rivers of pain

Rivers of regret

Rivers of fear

Lost

Found

Dumb

Educated

Broken

Repaired

Used

Anointed

Angry

Comforted

Sinner

Saved by grace

You've given silence when the noise was too loud

Calmness when chaos consumed

Dryness when soaked by tears

Webster doesn't have enough words to say sorry

Angered

Disappointed

Ignore

Ran

Diminished

Pretended

Praised – witness - prayed

Talked about worshipped knees bowed

Adored

Center of my joy

Creating a written vision that's plan

A miracle that's next

Finding something that's been sought

Opened that which had been knocked

Daily I fed myself of you

Not too late

Lost everything

Seesaw journey

Rollercoaster process

I fell in love with one who cannot lie

I remembered that love

When I though it left me

It lifted me up

When expecting punishment

You calmed the storm

Broken pieces have led to peace

Broken pieces – I've discovered the best peace in myself

There's a peace and confidence in the palm of my hands

Nailed…binded…hidden

You were my anchor all alone

You were in the midst all along

You admonished me…I should've received you

Submit to you now I'm in a midst of a shift

The lost things I've loved

I've lost folk I thought I wanted

I tried to hold on to what you wanted me away from

Pain at an all-time high

Fear at an all-time high

Despair at an all-time high

Vulnerability at an all-time high

Confidence is higher

Faith is higher

Motivation is higher

Self-forgiveness is higher

Focus is higher

I don't know what you're doing

Or where are you taking me

Broken and flawed as heck

You're using me for something

Not too low to grab

Not too dirty to clean up

Refreshed in my value

I succumb to the unknown

I succumb to who saved me

I succumb to what is healing me

Your voice I continue to hear

Your presence still consumes me

Your word still comforts me

Your grace and mercy

Renews and redeems

All pieces smooth yet ridged

Formed the IT, the BEING, the ONE…

…and in IT I am anchored.

Naked Truth 4: Faith

Always thought karma was my fan

I know faith hasn't loved me

Many times over I've chased it Bolt style

Many times not knowing if I'm coming or going

Determined and hurt

Pierced and inspired

Happy and torn

Lost and calm

Faith has taken me on one hell of a ride

I think I became a testament of faith

Before I even knew what it was

What pushed me to it

Kept me at the piano producing beautiful sounds

Or to stand in front of a microphone

Something soothing would come out

Angry and lost as a child

Always running away

Always running to

I knew something would make it better

Any problem…any need

What led me to know she'd always be there

December 2011

Pain…Perforation

Nurse said I'd be like this forever

I said you don't know what God I serve

Forever? Just 4 months

Faith

One moment it loves me

The next it beats me up

Daily I feed my body but I hadn't my faith

I honestly don't think I knew how

It was as if it was a dictionary on a shelf

Whenever I needed to know the meaning of a word

I'd go remove it

Disservice

Inadequate

Faith isn't a temporary fix

Nor a part time employee

Internalized

Embedded

It's a lifestyle choice

A gift

An avenue

Power source

We all possess

We all need to utilize

Limitless

Never running out

My darkest days found light

My heart remembered how to smile

Fear's hold loosened

Despair became distant

Favor? Reminded of

Peace amended

Shots will come

Shots will fly

Loads will become unbearable

Velcro adapts to what it is placed around

Faith adapts to what is placed before it.

Lemon Squeeze #1: Confessions

A huge fan but this ain't no Usher situation

Nothing salacious

Nothing exciting

Nothing messy nor revealing

A release

A moment of self-awareness

Outside of my head and therapy sessions

Although I have been hurt a million times over

I've hurt others as well

Intent wasn't negative

No maliciousness

Hurt is hurt and of it I'm guilty

I've lied, stolen, betrayed, manipulated

Never for personal gain

Desperation

Immaturity

No justification…I own it

All my life I've been chasing something

All my life I've been running away from something

I've ran to drugs, alcohol, sex to numb and hide pain

Feeling angry, lost, unworthy

I've never ran back to HIM first

I would run to anyone and anything

That allowed me to be my real self

The self I thought I needed to be

I've ran from family and actual real friends

Due to fear of judgement, neglect, unacceptance

Noises and thoughts in my head could get too loud

I'd run to anything to silence the noise

Hell sometimes I'd still do all of the above

I've been through a lot of pain in my life

Death and abuse have visited me frequently

Physical abuse as a child

Not the kind that leaves a little whelp

The kind that causes cuts and drippings of blood

The kind that leaves scars

I've been trusting the wrong people

From birth to year 38

Running to any kind of attention

Or anything I thought was love

Where did it get me?

Victim of sexual assault as a minor

Flashing lights and handcuffs as an adult

Alone many nights

Robbed

Lied about

Scandals

Disappointed

Cried enough tears to make me a personal lake

Betrayed, abused, abandoned by family

Used, abused, abandoned by friends

A multitude of negative experiences with frat

I got close to folks that I can say now…I absolutely don't like

Some of them niggas in my frat

Some of them in my family

Some have the privilege of saying I used to be their friend

Many of 'em? Life could leave them

I wouldn't care for a second

Now? Guarded with everyone breathing

Even the family, frat, friends I adore

Listen it hasn't all been bad

Growth

Healed

Partied

Some amazing times in my life

Forgiveness

Self-love

Self-acceptance

Take me or leave me

Either way success and achievement

Won't only be attached to my name

Deeply rooted in who I am

I have amazing friends

Some close than blood

Frat? Multiple ones huge motivators, supporters, and family

Relatives rather consistent or not

Plethora I appreciate and enjoy

No need for pity or sympathy

Love, respect, empathy is just fine

I'm in the midst of healing and evolution

Elevating and growing

Uncomfortable

At times a miserable transformation

Essential, bumpy, receptive journey

I release it

Nothing I've just mentioned can control me anymore

A part of my journey and story

Doesn't define me

Prayer, worship, hard work

Given me a written vision made plain

Grandma's hands

Spirit and love

Peace, calm, clarity

I'm alive

I'm free

I'm fighting

I'm not knocked out yet

I'm focused

I believe

I can

I will

I am!

Lemon Squeeze #2: Heal A Heart

Matters of the heart can be confusing

Many of us don't know the difference

Between what the brain or heart says vs. wants

Needs vs. Desires

The trauma it can go through

Bounces back

Has to be one of the strongest body parts

I'm numb to pain and tragedy

Experienced 'em too often

I don't want to constantly think about all its endured

I don't care to know how it can be

Broken and ripped apart

Yet still function

I just want to heal it

Disconnect between brain and heart is one issue

One has a plan

The other stops it from coming to fruition

One is fearless

One is strategic

Daily seesaw

One will wallow

One will keep it pushing

One will read you down

One will laugh and let it slide…once

Both resilient, petty, revengeful

Embracing all of it

Putting it to the left for a minute

How does a heart actually heal?

Forget the trauma and pain

I just want to heal my heart

I want my heart to smile again

I want my heart to feel joy again

Growth and healing of some degree

Have visited my heart

Fire and passion have poked my heart

Like Botox to my face during lunch break

How do I get through the last few meters in front of me?

Tired of feeling like nothing left

Hell…partially want to quit

From wanting to quit to laughing about quitting

Motivational seesaw

Fear and doubt in lanes 3 and 6

I'm lane 5

In other lanes are liquor, wrong friends, anger, despair

Satan is the wind blowing straight into me

Making it an uneasy task to finish this race

I don't want easy

I don't mind working had

I can excel under pressure

Not afraid of a little challenge

Neck and neck coming 'round the curve

10 meters left

I've moved ahead of liquor

I've moved passed wrong friends

My endurance seems to move me pass despair

Anger is right on my heels

Fear and doubt…we're neck and neck

I can't shake 'em

My heart syncopated

Warmth cascading through my veins

My heart? The central command center

Decisions to be made

Time running out

I see the finish line

Endurance and faith feeding oxygen into my body

My heart pieces leading me to peace

As my brain dwells in the secret place

It syncs with my heart and a transformation occurs

Temperature rises and falls

Veins erect with power and perseverance

Heart to heart…soul to soul

I don't desire the swift remedy

Longevity

Sustainable

Endurance to the end

This is one of many races

The difference is my team

The difference is my foundation remembered and strengthened

The difference is my truth

From broken and shattered

To bruised and sore

Weak and vulnerable

My heart is healing

My heart will go on

My heart is smiling

That awareness and growth

Now half of my battles have been won.

Broken Architect #2

The tears fall

No one is there to heed them

The heart? It mourns

No one sees the hurt

An emptiness has seeped into the brain stem

I'm feeling dazed

I'm no longer alert

Desolation haunts my whole persona

What can I do

Where can I go

Constantly feeling like I'm alone

Droplets

I'm often prompted

Unable to freely flow

Crying can be painful

Often crying for someone I loved so deeply

On the flip side grieving gives release

Only just a fraction

Slowly healing the ache

Seldom sadness is dismissed

Too slowly

Allegedly time eases sorrow

Directed to lean on faith and memories

Yet the drowning of each new day

Brings overwhelming feelings

Numbness

My hand swells

My heart shrinks

Blood runs through my veins icy cold

Blah feeling through the day

Blur knowledge of the day at end

Like a scale weighing kilos

Up and down are my emotions

A dime bag gets more love than me

2 kilos more valuable than my life

Like uncooked noodles sliding down a wall

So are 1,000 motivating words thrown at me

Choked by past mistakes

Whipped by fear

Starved by pain

Clawed by secrets

Suffering in silence

There's a ladder

I don't know if it's Jacob's or a stairway to heaven

My heart is tired and life could end

Wouldn't be missed

Written in the back of my mind

Then I remember faith

She never seemed to like me

Misunderstood mutually

There's something spiritual that keeps pulling at me

I want to run to it

I'd try anything at this point

Flashes of hope and determination

Flash in my brain like a marquee at the Staples Center

Standing in the midst of broken pieces

I see remnants of myself dangling

The one I'm afraid of could see me

The one I've clearly disappointed and angered

Could put these pieces back together

His way his time

Master and I servant

The created can't survive without the creator

Point blank period…I submit

I acknowledge

I cry out

I surrender and white is my new color

I succumb to your word and presence

No reasonable doubt

It's just you and me

So what are you going to do?

2130 Randolph Street

Oh if 2130 Randolph Street could talk

They may have changed your name to Pelham

But you will always be Randolph to me

When I entered the world

You were my first home

I've laid my head many places

But you were always my home

A lifelong connection

Predictable emotions

Love

Many lectures

Many prayers

Many worships

Many praises

Many gatherings

Some pain

Some heartaches

Some very tough moments

Rooted in unconditional love and

Unprecedented connection

SHE raised me there

My Queen

My heart

My everything

I learned my voice

Full transparency within those walls

No perfection but dedication

He did his best

She did the rest, did it all, kept that ship together

I am because she was

I can because she did

Oh 2130 – I got a lot of whoopings

Garage, my room, both living rooms

I've snuck in

Never snuck out

As a kid

All the land surrounding

Like my very own playground

As an adult

Not perfect

Who really cares for perfection

It was always a place of safety

Guarantees

Love

Sick with Crohn's at 13

I laid in her lap

Cried…didn't want to live

Stated I wanted to die

She held me in her lap

Wiped away all my tears

She hated to see me hurt

She hated to see me in pain

When I needed to rebuild

2007 summoned me

Many great meals and talks

We adored Kobe, Serena, Brandy

Watching them religiously

The nucleus for life's existence

2011 my body let me down

We didn't know what was wrong

What I did know was that I wanted her

What I did know is I wanted 2130

'Cause that's where she resided

At 2130 there was magical hugs

Truth telling

My foundation

I miss 2130

I will always miss 2130

When God took HER

2130 changed

In the midst of my lost and trauma

It deserted me

Anxiety

In the depth of my hell and pain

It healed me

One last time 2130 upheld me

Her spirit wrapped itself around me

Took from me what stalled my growth

At 2130 she always made things better

At 2130 I remembered to aid me and

Introduced me to my new normal

I don't know what the future holds

Some fear…lots of faith

Cheers to God

Cheers to Granny

Cheers to 2130 Randolph Street.

Here I Am Lord

She prayed to you for a reason

I was very young

When I saw how much you mattered to her

Many stories I was told

Some multiple times

You were a daily presence

I was introduced to you at a young age

Center of my joy

Order my steps

Comforted in the dark at 9

Soothed from physical abuse

Broken hearts

Shaky friends

Room full of family

Feeling lost and unloved

Many times I trusted people

More than I did you…idiotic me

Sex, drugs, alcohol

Over faith, praise, patience

Damaged

Prodigal son

Many examples of your power and consistency

Yet I failed

I failed you

I disappointed you

I disobeyed you

Multiple times ended up afraid of you

Feeling unworthy

Take me Jesus

I'm tired of pain

I'm tired of hurting

I want my smile to not just be on my face

But my heart

Crying out for redemption

Forgive me

Broken rules, sins, wasted blessings

Wash me anew

Use me for your purpose

Bruised, battered, broken

I come to you

Opened and surrendered

My mistakes won't define me

Grace and mercy…resolution to a closed case

You're not in the business of wasting blessings

So here I am at a place

I thought would never be

Progression unbelieved or felt I'd deserve

You've given me healing

I always said if only I could

Have half the faith she did

Unprecedented transformation would come

Not sure if I'm there yet

Your everlasting arm I lean on daily

I talk to you multiple times a day

It's just me and you

I'm the clay…you're the potter

My better me is being molded

I've impacted others more than myself

I've enriched others more than myself

I've loved others more than myself

Favored…forgiven

Her prayers kept me

Had it not been

But for the grace of God

Her prayers

I'd be like a ship without a sail

A song without a writer

A country without a leader

A car without an engine

The devil had me for a while

I shout until water comes out of the rock

I'm a pray until the seas part

Your oil more powerful than his hold

I need you now

Every day is like a battle…a task

I want to go where you lead me

I want to be what you want me to be

All my life

Running to and from something

Tired…no more

No matter what

Wash me

Cleanse me

Here I am Lord…I'm yours!

Who I Was

A shift has come and it's here

I am who I am

Beautifully imperfect

I've loved hard and I've loved long

I've forgiven and been forgiven

I haven't always forgiven when I should've

I've hurt when I should've loved

I've kept quiet when I should've spoken

Flip sides

I was heard when

Everything reoccurring

I should've just been seen

I am who I am

I am not who I was

I'm moving different

I want different

Old keys can't unlock new doors

Everything I'm requiring

I'm reciprocating

If you remember anything about me

When it's all said and done

I loved when it was foolish

Gave to others

Nothing to give myself

Fed others when internally I was starving

I've cared when it was unwanted

When my body is gone

Remember my heart

I am being stronger than my excuses

I am who I am

Not who I was

I have been shackled

I have been judged

Stabbed in the back

Knife turned in all directions

I've had valley and mountain top experiences

I've had breakthroughs and blessings

Achievements and celebrations

Judged and loved

Abandoned and neglected

I've lashed out, stolen from, deserted

Revengeful

I've cried, fought, nurtured

Lied and kept secrets

Even made some amends

When it mattered to me

I am who I am

Not who I was.

Leave Me The F**K Alone

For most of my life

I was so consumed with validation

Wrong areas

Not any right areas

I wanted to be acknowledged by folk

Loved

Wanted

Surrounded

Needed

Now? I just want to be left the f**k alone

What I require I reciprocate

My loyalty to the end…have it

My prayers and support…have it

An alibi? I got you

A ride or die? Let's get it

Yes men boil my blood

You thrive off of 'em

You can keep 'em

Who you think you are is rooted in yes men

Mine rooted in truth and discernment

Many not aware of the saying

It's better to be seen and not heard

Your place and your lane…important

Want problems? Step out of your lane

Family? Some blessings

Others thorns in my side

Friends have come and go

The right ones still remain

People purge I love

Shifts are healthy

Every situationship isn't meant to last forever

Mission done

Many folk experienced bad decisions

My bad decisions

Assuming folk changed

Letting folks close to me

That multiple times I'd normally cut off

Some of an organizational affiliation broke me

Damaged me

Lied and betrayed

Like an idiot I remained loyal

Gotten to a point of no return

My lack of emotional attachment is deeply rooted

My distance sustainable

Do right by me or

Leave me the f**k alone

I have been crucified

For what others have been celebrated for

They do it? Swept under a rug

I do it or perception of? World War 3

Physical and mental abuse…an audience brings no rescuer

Followed folk to the ends of the earth

Kept their secrets

An effective fixer

Listen to conversations I cared nothing about

Kept quiet to feed their sensitivity and lack of accountability

Removing wool over my eyes

Ignored the right people

Hindsight 20/20

Fed the weakest links

Loving and yearning for attention

I gave way more than was needed

Took too long to not just see but act

I did a disservice to myself

No experience or knowledge of

Keep your advice

Carries no weight

Long list of folks I've upheld

Supported

Rode and died with

Who was present

My list when I needed someone

Shorter than the hair on a newborn baby

Public service announcement

Warning

Disclaimer

Do right by me or leave me the f**k alone!

I Bow Out

<u>Act 1</u>

It was dark and I searched for you

I prayed to you

Called for you

Cried out to you

I heard nothing

24 hours in a day

2 years of constant hell

Choking on fears, despair, tears

Yet still…could've been worse

You're present but you're quiet

Looking left and right

Obviously you're present

Why won't you answer me

Why won't you rescue me

I fasted

I told people about you

Changes made

Growth initiated

Crowd shrunk

Relationships cease and desist

Relationships' quality increased

Loved myself

Negligence no more

Fed myself with you daily

Good or bad – I praised you

3 years suffocating

Why haven't I heard from you

Why haven't you rescued me

I'm not ungrateful

I'm not selfish

I'm unworthy and afraid

No ideations but…

…I don't want to be here

She's stronger

They're fine without me

They'll heal better than I can

I heal others

But can't heal myself

I just want to hear from you

Rescue me

Or finally my encore has 1 final reprise

A round of applause…my last curtain call……

<u>Act 2</u>

Ya'll can have all this shit

This passion

These goals

These problems

These burdens

These dreams

This life

I don't want to hear nothing 'bout

No damn strength, comeback, or what you see in me

It's all a day late and a dollar short

The Ra'Mone that you've known

The me that you've experienced

The I that you've loved

Has been dead for some time

No time wasted with a funeral

Cremated

Where are the ashes

I signed an NDA with my soul

Lips are sealed……

<u>Act 3</u>

Am I he me really dead

Or has dead weight been shed

Do I know the difference

Have shackles been broken

Have I been broken, burned, and torn

So that my heart, mind, and soul

Could get some much needed surgery

I honestly don't give a damn what it is

One thing for sure

2 things for certain

My mind needs rest

My soul needs peace

I just want my heart to smile again

So bags packed

Paperwork signed

Cut fresh

Tape tight

Dreads put up

Headed to the place

Headed to perform

One last time……

<u>Act 4</u>

On my left you whispered REVERSE

On my right you whispered…YOU'RE NO MORE –
NOTHING LEFT TO GIVE

The right consumed me

It spoke to my mind

I walked in

Stood out front and center

Reminiscing

It left me

It touched me

I don't know what or who it was

Relief

Load not as heavy

Broken hearted pieces moving

My heart connected to something

I'd never experienced

Transformation destination

Release flowed from me

The left and right got louder

Pills and liquor awaited me

On the other side of the wall

I've done all I can

I give up

Never been a quitter

Content with being one today

Notifications given

I walked closer to the wall

Resolution a few feet away

Stopped in my tracks

This feeling pulled at my heart

Water works had been flowing over 30 minutes

A hand on my shoulder

A presence wrapped around me like a tornado

Change of plans

I've visited trouble

Now I'm ready for it

Calmness in the air

Temperature changed

No longer a tug a war I was losing

A connection with my heart upholding me

The journey and story not yet finished

This is my reprise

The last and only reprise

That doesn't mean there can't be a remix

I learned from the best

It's my business

It's my journey

I won't keep up an act

No games to be played

Life or death

One more push

The melody has finished

So I'm looking to you…carry me forth.

My Invitation

I never strived for perfection

Progression was my goal

It is clear I was never in control

No matter the changes

No matter the plans

No matter the growth

No matter the evolution

It was never enough

I never had the final say

I need a full audit

My multiple assessment clearly incomplete

I open my heart

I open my mind

I commune with you

Spirit to spirit

An unending invitation

To the deepest depths of my soul

Rooted in my transition position

I want to be blessed so I can bless others

Providing for self

Allows for a level of service to others

In your name…that gives me joy

I open my heart

I open my mind

I commune with you

Spirit to spirit

An unending invitation

To the deepest depths of my soul

You can give it to me

I have strength enough to use it

My request isn't for me alone

My village…my team…strangers

Let the connection flow from me

I have an inquiry

A new perspective

Some selfishness may be needed

He who keeps me

Can keep them too

I'm sustaining myself a top priority

Obligation and objective

I've given more of myself to others than to myself

More of myself to others than to you

Over depleted myself for others

Got to my destination with nothing in the tank

I open my heart

I open my mind

I commune with you

Spirit to spirit

An unending invitation

To the deepest depths of my soul

I'm reversing the language

So you can reverse my life

Where you're leading me

Everyone can't go

Many don't want revelation

They want attention

Forced…essential

Learned how to let folk in my life

Not in my spirit

I could freakin' give up right now

No matter how bad I wanted to

You wouldn't let me

You wouldn't make it easier

You wouldn't let me give up

No peace

You wouldn't let me give up

No lesser load

You wouldn't let me give up

I felt teased and tortured by you and life

I couldn't fight it

I couldn't hide from it

I couldn't run from it

I couldn't transfer or return to sender

Like I said I was never in control

Never had the final say

After you've done all you can just stand…

…I AINT HAVE NANN STAND LET IN ME – PERIOD

3 years in hell and torture

No break nor relief

I could either continue being consumed by the brokenness

Despair and defeat

Or just give in to the massa

I open my heart

I open my mind

I commune with you

Spirit to spirit

An unending invitation

To the deepest depths of my soul.

Awareness and Blessings

Submissiveness, humility, and acceptance

For every mountain – for every…

Slap

Cut

Fistula

Tear

Nightmare

Dream

Awareness and blessings – I thank you

For every…

Flaw

Hug

Solo

Prayer

Speech

Piano key pressed

Kiss

Handshake

Awareness and blessings — I thank you

For every…

Drop from my eye

Smile

Orgasm

Lesson

Heartbreak

Hospitalization

Job

Class

Degrees

Termination

Awareness and blessings — I thank you

For every…

Current friend

Terminated friend

Disappointment

Book

Movie

Song

Lie

Enricher

Motivator

Award

Rumor

Mistake

Breakthrough

Awareness and blessings – I thank you

For every…

Valley

Dark night

Depression episode

2 Failed suicide attempts

Trip

Drink

Nourishment

Argument

Moment of loneliness

Grief period

Abandonment

Abuse

Laugh

Tea spilled

Awareness and blessings – I thank you

For every…

Philanthropy effort

No

Yes

Shut door

Betrayal

Neglect

Fulfillment

Rescue

Second of grace

Moment of mercy

Awareness and blessings – I thank you

For every…

Scripture

Step

Exercise

Home

Relative

Scar

Car

Event

Elevation

Troubled fear

Doubt

Doubter

Flame

Demon

Passion

Enemy

Joy

Forgiveness

Peace

AWARENESS AND BLESSINGS – I THANK YOU!

About The Author

Ra'Mone Marquis is a southern gentleman, born and raised in Florida. Life experiences and literary idols such as Omar Tyree, Terry McMillan, and Eric Jerome Dickey; have shaped Ra'Mone into the author that he is today. This is what formed the foundation of him being a refreshing literary artist with high levels of uniqueness and relatability.

Seeing a need in his community, specifically with that of minority youth, Ra'Mone started his 501c3 foundation – Tru Phoenix Foundation, LLC. (formerly True T.A.L.E.N.T.S. Foundation, Inc.) Since its inception in 2011, this foundation has served a plethora of minority youth in the central and south Florida areas through its mentoring conference, mentoring sessions, and various initiatives.

Courtesy of his company Tru Phoenix, LLC., formally Kace Books, LLC., he has released 4 written works that are all 5-star reviewed and have reached the Amazon Bestsellers List. They are District 69: The Crimson Edition, District 69: The Color Haven, District 69: The Greek Chronicles, and his first #1 book A Poetic Exhale. All books are available on Kindle, Amazon, Nook, ibooks, and more. Ra'Mone is also the host of his own podcast, The QB Zone. All episodes are available on Iheartradio, Spotify, Apple Podcasts, Google Podcasts, and Audible; video episodes available on the YouTube channel: Quis Box.

<u>Contact Info:</u>

Website: www.ramonemarquisofficial.com

Instagram: @ramonemarquis

Twitter: @ramonemarquis

Facebook: Ra'Mone Marquis